THE GREAT BIG
WATER CYCLE
ADVENTURE

All inquiries should be addressed to:
Barron's Educational Series, Inc.
250 Wireless Boulevard
Hauppauge, NY 11788
www.barronseduc.com

ISBN: 978-1-4380-5044-7

Library of Congress Control Number:
2017958565

Date of Manufacture: February 2018
Manufactured by: WKT Co., Ltd.,
Shenzhen, China

Printed in China
9 8 7 6 5 4 3 2 1

THE GREAT BIG
WATER CYCLE
ADVENTURE

Written by
Kay Barnham

Illustrated by
Maddie Frost

BARRON'S

Did you know that the same water has been falling as raindrops for billions of years? It travels around our planet, again and again. The journey it takes is called the water cycle.

Are you ready to dive into the great
big water cycle story?

The sun is a very important part of the water cycle.

When the hot sun shines on our planet, the water in oceans and seas becomes warmer. As this happens, the water changes from liquid into a gas called vapor.

The water vapor rises because it is warm. As the vapor travels higher, it cools and changes from an invisible gas into tiny droplets of water and ice.

When the tiny droplets join together, clouds form.

As more and more droplets stick to each other, they grow bigger and bigger.

The droplets in the clouds become too big and heavy to stay in the air.

The water droplets then fall back to Earth as rain, hail, sleet, and snow.

When water lands on our planet,
its never-ending journey continues.
Where does it go next? This depends
on where the water falls...

If water falls into the oceans and seas, the water cycle starts all over again.

If water falls on land,
some of it runs over
the surface and trickles
into streams.

Small streams join larger streams. These flow into rivers. Some rivers and streams tumble and gush down mountainsides as waterfalls.

This water travels back to the sea.

Some water falls or runs into ponds, lakes, and reservoirs. This water may flow onward to the sea. The sun may turn it into vapor again, or the water may stay put for many years.

When summers
are long and hot, more
water turns into vapor.
Lakes and rivers disappear.

Water will also fall onto plants and trees. It may trickle to the ground and get soaked up by plant roots. This helps plants grow.

Water droplets on leaves
are warmed by the sun
and turn back into vapor.

Some water falls on land and seeps
deep down underground. It then fills
the cracks and gaps between
soil, sand, and rock.

This groundwater moves slowly. It takes a long time to return to the sea.

Other times, water
falls as snow. When it
lands on mountaintops and in
cold places, it does not melt
at once. It may take a very long
time to return to the sea.

Some of the world's water has been frozen
for thousands of years. It is trapped in glaciers,
which are slow-moving rivers of ice.

The water cycle does not
always run smoothly.

When there is too much rain, the water
builds up too fast and there are floods.

When too little rain falls, there is less water in streams and rivers. This can lead to droughts.

Did you know that most of the water on our planet is salty seawater? Only a small amount is the freshwater we need to survive.

Over seven billion people live on our planet. By using less water, we can make sure that there is enough for everyone.

The Great Big Water Cycle Adventure never ends. Follow the arrows to see how water goes around and around...

clouds form,

The sun warms our planet,

water vapor rises,

water droplets
fall back to Earth,

streams and rivers
carry water back to the
sea. Groundwater travels
slowly back to the sea, and
water is stored in oceans,
ice caps, underground,
and in the atmosphere.

THINGS TO DO

1. Use watercolors to paint your own water cycle picture! Add arrows to show how water travels around and around.

2. Make a water cycle game. Write a different stage of the water cycle, such as WATER VAPOR RISES, CLOUDS FORM, and RAIN FALLS on individual squares. Roll dice to move your counters around the board.

3. Create a word cloud about water! Write "water" in the middle of the page. Next, add all the words that this word makes you think of. Write them all down using different colored pens. Start like this...

SEA WATER RAIN

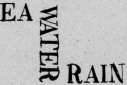

NOTES FOR PARENTS AND TEACHERS

This series aims to encourage children to look at and wonder about different aspects of the world in which they live. Here are some specific ideas for getting more out of this book:

1. Encourage children to observe how the water cycle works. Leave a tray outside and watch as it fills with rain. On a sunny day, observe how the sun's heat makes the water evaporate.

2. Put on a play in which children pretend to be a water droplet traveling through all the stages of the water cycle.

3. Decorate a paper plate to show the different stages of the water cycle. Spin the plate to show how the water cycle goes around and around.

4. Ask children about saving water. How many different ways can they think of to save water?

5. Can children guess how much water is wasted from a dripping faucet? To find out, ask them to carry out an experiment by measuring how much water is collected in a cup after one hour.

WATER CYCLE BOOKS TO SHARE

Water Is Water: A Book About the Water Cycle
by Miranda Paul
(Roaring Brook Press, 2015)

A Drop Around the World
by Barbara McKinney and Michael S. Maydak
(Dawn Publications, 1998)

All the Water in the World
by George Ella Lyon and Katherine Tillotson
(Atheneum/Richard Jackson Books, 2011)

National Geographic Readers: Water
by Melissa Stewart
(National Geographic Children's Books, 2014)